Copyright © 2025 by Charlotte Chang

All rights reserved. No part of this publication may be reproduced, distributed, or transmitted in any form or by any means, including photocopying, recording, or other electronic or mechanical methods, without the prior written permission of the publisher, except in the case of brief quotations embodied in critical reviews and certain other noncommercial uses permitted by copyright law.

ISBN 978-1-998317-93-6

Cover design by Charlotte Chang.

First Edition: November, 2025

Lady Yin was pregnant for a very,
very long time.
One night, she gave birth to a shiny ball.
Li Jing opened it, and a baby boy came out.
His name was Nezha.

殷夫人怀孕了很久很久。
一天晚上,她生下了一颗亮晶晶的大圆球。
李靖小心地打开圆球,
里面蹦出一个可爱的小男孩。
他们给他取名叫哪吒。

An immortal named Taiyi Zhenren flew down from the clouds.
He said, "Nezha is a magical child."
He taught Nezha magic and gave him a gold ring and a red ribbon.

一位名叫太乙真人的神仙从云端飞来。
他说:"哪吒是个有灵气的孩子。"
太乙真人教哪吒练本领,
还送给他两件法宝:乾坤圈和混天绫。

Nezha grew fast.
He loved splashing, running,
and playing by the wide blue sea.

nǎ zhā hěn kuài cháng dà le
哪吒很快长大了。
tā zuì xǐ huān dào lán lán de dà hǎi biān wán shuǐ
他最喜欢到蓝蓝的大海边玩水、
bēn pǎo hé wán shuǎ
奔跑、和玩耍。

One day, a fierce Yaksha came out of the water.
He pointed at Nezha.
"You! Come to the Dragon Palace!"

一天，一名凶巴巴的夜叉从海里窜出来。
他指着哪吒大喊：
"你！跟我到龙宫来！"

Nezha shook his head.
The Yaksha rushed at him.
Nezha jumped aside
and swung his gold ring.
With a bright flash,
the Yaksha turned into light
and went back into the sea.

哪吒摇摇头,不肯去。
夜叉立刻扑了上来。
哪吒一跳,轻轻闪开,
举起乾坤圈用力一挥。
只见一道亮光闪过,
夜叉变成一束光影,
一下子又跌回了海里。

Ao Bing rose from the waves.
"Come with me!" he said.
Nezha refused.

They fought in swirling water and wind.
Nezha used his red ribbon,
and Ao Bing turned into shining light
and disappeared.

敖丙从海里冒出来，
对哪吒说："跟我走！"
哪吒还是不答应。
海水和风一起旋转起来，两人打成一团。
哪吒甩出红色的混天绫，轻轻一绕，
敖丙化成一束亮光，慢慢消失在海里。

The Dragon King rushed toward Heaven
to make a complaint.
But Nezha flew up to stop him on the way.
The Dragon King grew even angrier.
"Fine! I will flood the land!"

Dark clouds rolled in.
The sea began to rise.

龙王气冲冲地去天宫告状。
哪吒立刻飞起来拦住他。
龙王更生气了:
"好！那我就放大水！"

乌云滚滚，
海水也开始慢慢升高。

Huge waves crashed onto the shore.
People ran in fear.
The water kept getting higher and higher.

巨大的海浪扑到岸边。
村里的人吓得赶紧往高处跑。
海水越涨越高。

Nezha watched the rising sea.
He knew the trouble came from him.
"I must stop this," he said.
He made a brave choice.

哪吒望着不断上涨的海水，
他知道是自己惹的祸。
"我得想办法让它停下来。"
于是，他做出了一个勇敢的决定。

Nezha held all his magic inside.
Bright white light wrapped around him.
He slowly turned into a soft white glow
and drifted away.
The sea became quiet again.

哪吒把法力往回收,
一圈白光慢慢把他包住。
他的身体渐渐变得很轻,
化成一束温暖的白光,慢慢飘向远处。
海面逐渐回归平静了。

That night, Taiyi Zhenren came
to Lady Yin in a dream.
"Build a small temple for Nezha," he said.

Lady Yin built it with love.
People came to say thank you.

那天夜里,太乙来到了殷夫人的梦里。
他说:"给哪吒建一座小庙吧。"
殷夫人满心想念,就细心地把庙建好了。
村里的人也陆续前来致谢。

Taiyi Zhenren gathered lotus roots and petals.
With magic, he made a new body.
Soft, bright, and glowing.
A spark of light flew inside.

Nezha opened his eyes.

太乙真人采来莲藕和花瓣,
用法力给哪吒做了一个新的身体,
柔柔的、亮亮的,还闪着光。
接着,一缕光飞进身体。
哪吒慢慢睁开了眼睛。

Nezha returned to his hometown.
He saw his family again.
People cheered for him.
From then on, Nezha protected his home,
and everyone loved their brave young hero.

nǎ zhā huí dào le jiā xiāng
哪吒回到了家乡。
tā yòu jiàn dào le zì jǐ de jiā rén
他又见到了自己的家人。
cūn lǐ de rén kàn jiàn nǎ zhā píng ān huí lái
村里的人看见哪吒平安回来，
dōu gāo xìng dì pāi shǒu huān hū
都高兴地拍手欢呼。
cóng nà yǐ hòu nǎ zhā yī zhí shǒu hù zhe tā men
从那以后，哪吒一直守护着他们，
dà jiā yě gèng jiā xǐ huān zhè gè yǒng gǎn de xiǎo yīng xióng
大家也更加喜欢这个勇敢的小英雄。

www.ingramcontent.com/pod-product-compliance
Lightning Source LLC
LaVergne TN
LVHW070453080526
838202LV00035B/2821